Roger,

We know you've been filled with thoughts about the kind of dad you want to be. Here are a few more ideas to add to the ■■■■■■■■k "Hearts of Rhea ■■■■■■ - top the list!

Love,
Martha Roger

Just Dads

Just
DADS

*Nerves of Steel,
Wills of Iron,
Hearts of Pudding*

compiled by
Bonnie Louise Kuchler

Willow Creek®
P R E S S

Published by Willow Creek Press
P.O. Box 147, Minocqua, Wisconsin 54548
For information on other Willow Creek Press titles, call 1-800-850-9453 or visit us on the web at www.willowcreekpress.com.

Design: Pat Linder
Editor: Andrea Donner

Library of Congress Cataloging-in-Publication Data
Just dads : nerves of steel, wills of iron, hearts of pudding / compiled by Bonnie Louise Kuchler.
    p. cm.
  ISBN 1-57223-509-8 (hardcover : alk. paper)
1. Fathers--Quotations, maxims, etc. 2. Fatherhood--Quotations, maxims, etc. I. Kuchler, Bonnie Louise.
  PN6084.F3 J87 2002
  306.874'2--dc21

                                                    2002001084

Printed in Canada

*In memory of my dad, who showed me
the importance of butterfly kisses.*

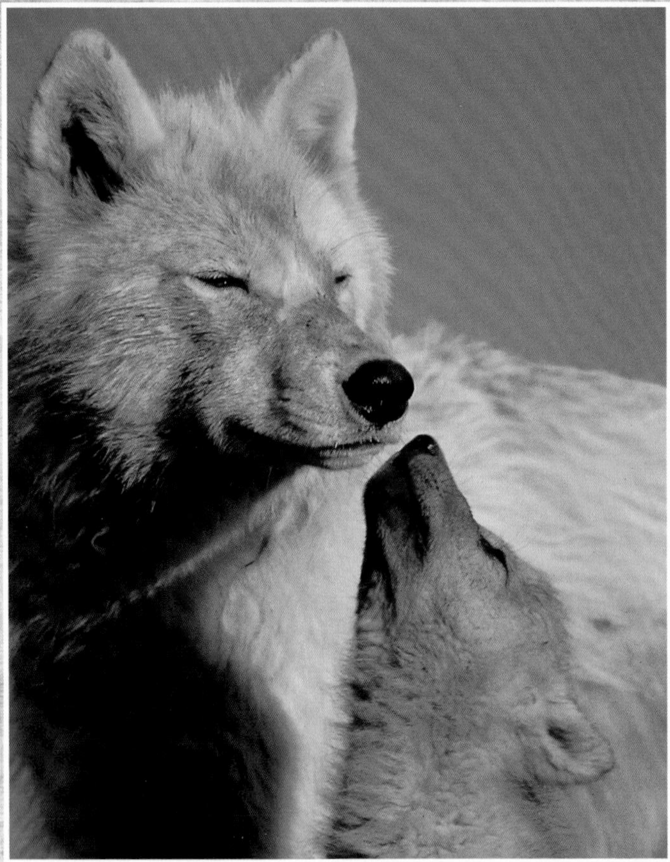

Acknowledgements

Thanks to Ken Sikes, the father of my children, who has given my daughter a sense of security only a loving father can impart, who has helped my son find his way in this mixed-up world, and who has taught them both a mean game of Scrabble.

Thanks also to Pat Linder, artist extraordinaire, for creating such delightful covers for my books. And thanks to Andrea Donner, sagacious editor, for believing in my first book enough to let me do another.

Nothing could get me if I curled up on my father's lap . . .
all about him was safe.

Naomi Mitchison (1897-1999)
British author

Emperor Penguin: The Emperor Penguin is different than all other penguins because it breeds in winter rather than summer, and incubates its egg without making a nest in temperatures well below zero by balancing the egg carefully on its feet. After mating, the female lays one egg and after a few days of passing it back and forth with her mate, she leaves the egg with the father for incubation while she goes off to feed. Hundreds of males stand beak-to-back for six weeks, each incubating an egg. Huddled to keep warm in subzero temperatures and icy winds, the birds form a huge circular group called a "tortue." The group slowly spirals, with males on the outside shuffling slowly toward the center. In this way, each dad takes his turn as a windbreak so that all may survive. During this time, the male birds eat nothing and lose nearly half their body weight. The chicks usually hatch just as the females return. The mothers feed them a meal of regurgitated food. If Mom is late, Dad can feed the chick for a few days with a protein-rich milk produced in his gullet. On her return, the mother takes over the task of caring for the chick for the next few weeks while the father goes to sea to feed and recover. After that, the chick is fed by both parents.

Every day of my life had been a gift from him.

from poem "My Father's Best Gift"

Seahorse: Male seahorses have a special pouch on their bellies into which their mates lay their eggs. Dad's brood pouch swells like a balloon during the several-week incubation. He literally "gives birth" to about 150 babies by tightening the muscles in his pouch until one by one the diminutive seahorses pop out through a small opening. Not one to waste precious time, the female "impregnates" the male again the minute the first brood is delivered.

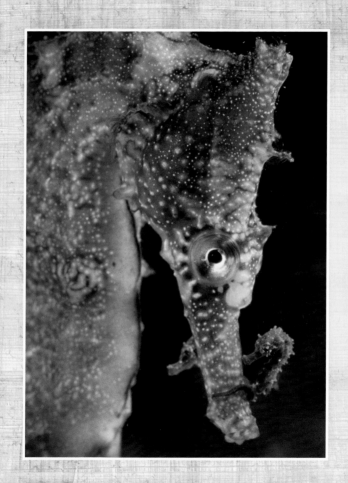

Fathers have a special excitement about them
that babies find intriguing . . .
Fathers embody a delicious mixture
of familiarity and novelty.

LOUISE J. KAPLAN
20th-century American psychologist

Lion: At night, a male lion patrols and marks his territory, claiming his turf with a series of loud roars. The roar of a lion can be heard up to five miles away and is quite intimidating. The father's job is to defend the pride against other marauding lions or predators that would steal food or kill his cubs.

[Fatherhood] is the single most creative, complicated, fulfilling, frustrating, engrossing, enriching, depleting endeavor of a man's adult life.

KYLE D. PRUETT
author, child development expert

Common Loon: Male loons help with all aspects of raising young, as is true of most bird species that mate for life. The pair winters separately but reunite on northern lakes in the spring. After over a month of courting and jointly preparing a nest near the water's edge, the female lays two eggs. Both parents share the month-long incubation and care for the chicks. Loon chicks can swim almost immediately, but spend some time on their parents' backs to rest, conserve heat, and avoid predators. Chicks are fed exclusively by their protective parents for the first few weeks of life, and until they are about eight weeks old.

It is much easier to become a father than to be one.

KENT NERBURN
theologian

Coyote: Coyote pairs often mate for life. While the female nurses young pups in the den, the male will stand guard, hunt, and bring food back for his mate. Once the pups are weaned, both parents hunt to feed them, and both parents lead them away from the den and show them how to catch mice or rabbits.

*We never know the love of the parent 'till
we become parents ourselves.*

REVEREND HENRY WARD BEECHER (1813-1887)

Trumpeter Swan: Together the swan pair constructs a large mound-shaped nest with twigs and bits of plant materials from the bottom of the nearest body of water. The male helps some with incubation when the female goes to feed, but she is the primary incubator. The day after the new swans (cygnets) have hatched, the adults lead them into the water. The cygnets are able to swim and to peck at green particles of floating duckweed or tiny snails where the water is shallow. The mother and father stay in close attendance and will sometimes pump their big webbed feet up and down to loosen small bits of food for the cygnets. As the family swims along, the mother leads the novice swimmers while the father paddles behind, ever watchful. He chases off intruders, hissing and beating his powerful wings.

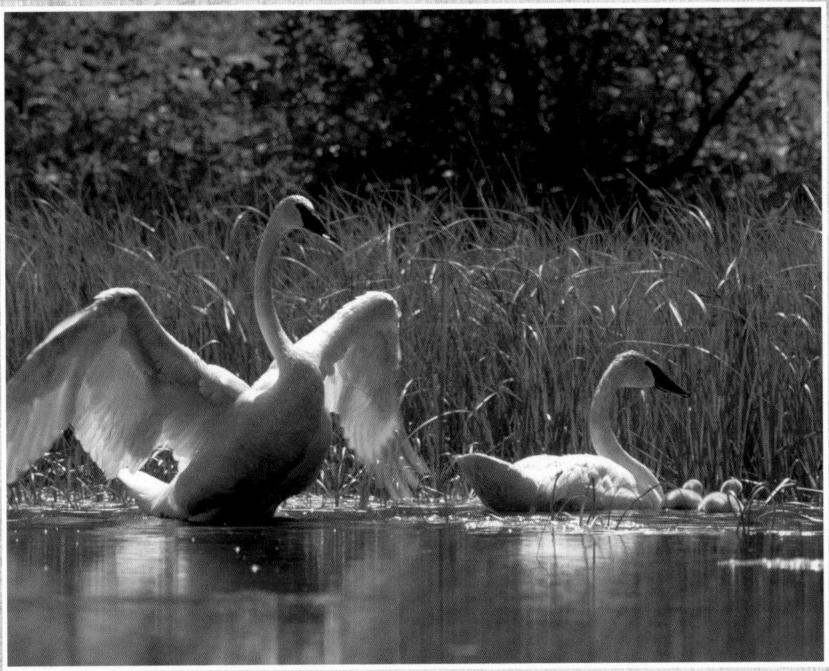

A real family man is one who can look at his new child as an addition rather than a deduction.

ANONYMOUS

Baboon: An adult male baboon plays a "godfather role" to a female's offspring, whether he is the real father or not. This "consort" will play with, groom, and carry the infant. He also is quick to protect her young, preventing other animals from taking the baby from its mother. Male consorts may even become foster parents if the mother dies.

The truth is, one's vocation is never some far-off possibility.—It is always the simple round of duties which the passing hour brings.

JOHN WELCH DULLES (1823-1887)
American clergyman and educator

Common Kingfisher: Kingfishers nest in underground burrows usually in the banks of rivers. At the end of a six-foot long tunnel, the mated pair builds a large, round chamber where the female lays her eggs. The male and female take turns incubating them, and both parents feed the chicks for the first four weeks of their lives. After that, the female leaves to find another burrow, leaving the male to feed the fledglings while they learn to catch fish, insect larvae, and tadpoles. As the chicks grow, the father will bring them fish less and less frequently, and after about two months, the young birds are fully independent.

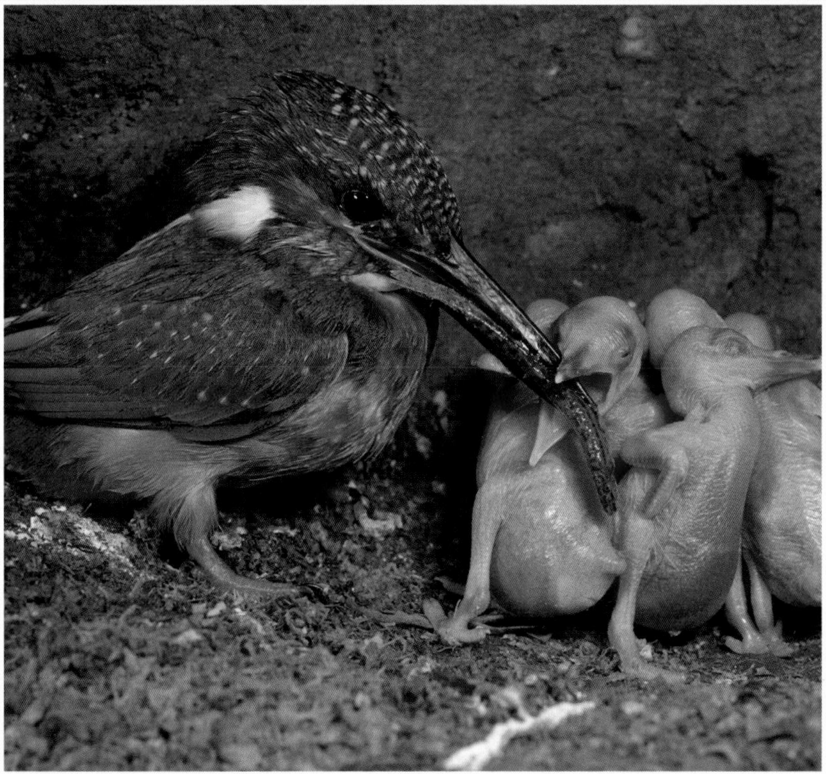

A perfect example of minority rule
is a baby in the house.

ANONYMOUS

Bush (or Rock) Hyrax: Rock Hyraxes live in family groups of one adult male, several adult females, and their offspring, and all cooperate in caring for the young. The rabbit-sized hyraxes are native to Africa where they live only among rocks where there are plenty of nooks and crannies in which to hide. The male is always on lookout duty. If he utters a sharp cry of alarm, all dash for cover and remain frozen until the danger passes.

A baby will make love stronger,
days shorter, nights longer,
bankroll smaller, home happier,
clothes shabbier, the past forgotten,
and the future worth living for.

ANONYMOUS

Prairie Dog: Prairie dog towns are made up of webs of tunnels and burrows that form a vast city containing thousands of animals. Separate family groups, or coteries, of eight or nine animals live in their own space within the city. Prairie dogs are highly social, maintaining their social structure with a ritual of "kisses" (they touch noses in greeting). Pups spend most of their time at play, and adults of both sexes tolerate their antics and often join in their fun.

Prairie dogs eat away all the tall plants in their vicinity so that ground predators, such as ferrets and weasels, have nowhere to hide. A sentry, often a male, keeps watch and if he spots a predator approaching, will stand up on his back legs and bark toward the sky. This call of alarm will be echoed by the other lookout dogs until the warning has spread throughout the entire town. Once the danger has passed, the dog gives an "all clear" signal by jumping in the air and throwing back his head, yipping.

If the new American father feels bewildered and even defeated, let him take comfort from the fact that whatever he does in any fathering situation has a fifty percent chance of being right.

BILL COSBY

Gray Wolf: Wolves live in packs, wherein each member is part of an extended family with a strict social order. The leaders are the dominant male and female, and all other animals submit to them. Normally, only the dominant male and female breed. The female gives birth to 5 or 6 pups that are dependent on the pack members for food until they are several months old. The subordinate members of the pack, whether male or female, help in the task of raising the pups. If a pup licks a helper's face as it returns from hunting, the pup will be given regurgitated food. Helpers will also guard the young while the other adults go hunting. All of the pack members, including the dominant male and female, will let the puppies climb on them and play. As the pups grow, the entire pack will teach them how to survive.

Reasoning with a two-year-old is about as productive as changing seats on the Titanic.

ROBERT SCOTELLARO

Great Blue Heron: Great Blue Herons become quite social during the nesting season, with each pair building a two- to three-foot-wide stick nest close to others in the spreading crowns of a few huge trees. In a ritualized display, the male gathers sticks and gives them to the female, who adds them to the previous year's nest or constructs a new nest. Once the eggs are laid, both parents incubate the eggs and share in defending their territory. Once hatched, the young are first fed soft, regurgitated food directly into their mouths from both parents. Later, whole fish are regurgitated into the nest. By the end of three weeks, the young grab their parents' bills to stimulate the regurgitation.

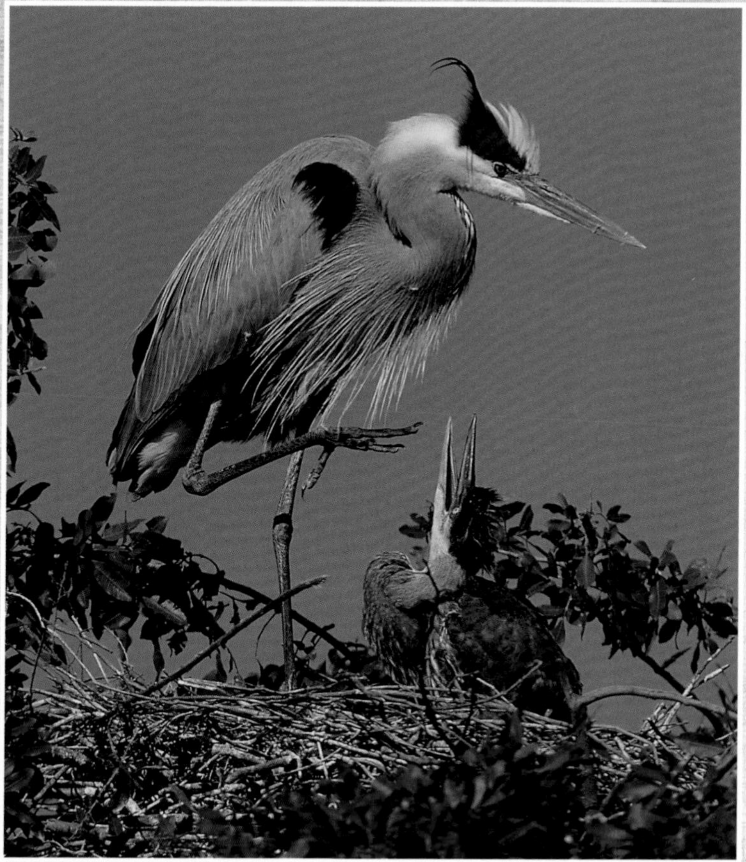

Scary. That may be the most perfect word there is to describe what it's like to be a parent.

D. L. STEWART
20th century American author

White Helmet Shrike: Both adult shrikes work at building their nest, although the male tends to carry more nest material while the female is the primary constructor. During the nesting season, shrikes store food by skewering insects and small mammals on thorns or barbed wire fences. They create a larder of food so that the male can feed the incubating female and so that both parents can feed the chicks once they hatch. After hatching, the ever-hungry nestling shrikes eat so many insects that it takes both parents to keep them supplied with enough food. Although the fledglings try to catch their own food, they are very awkward fliers and not very good at catching insects. Thus, the parents continue to feed them until the young shrikes have become proficient hunters.

*Fatherhood is the most courageous
of all occupations.*

W.H. MERTZ III

Lion: Cubs will play with the tufted tail of their father and occasionally use Dad as a portable playground. An adult male may pull a few grimacing faces or show disapproval with a hissing sound, but generally he tolerates the cubs even when the youngsters play with his food and try to take food out of his mouth.

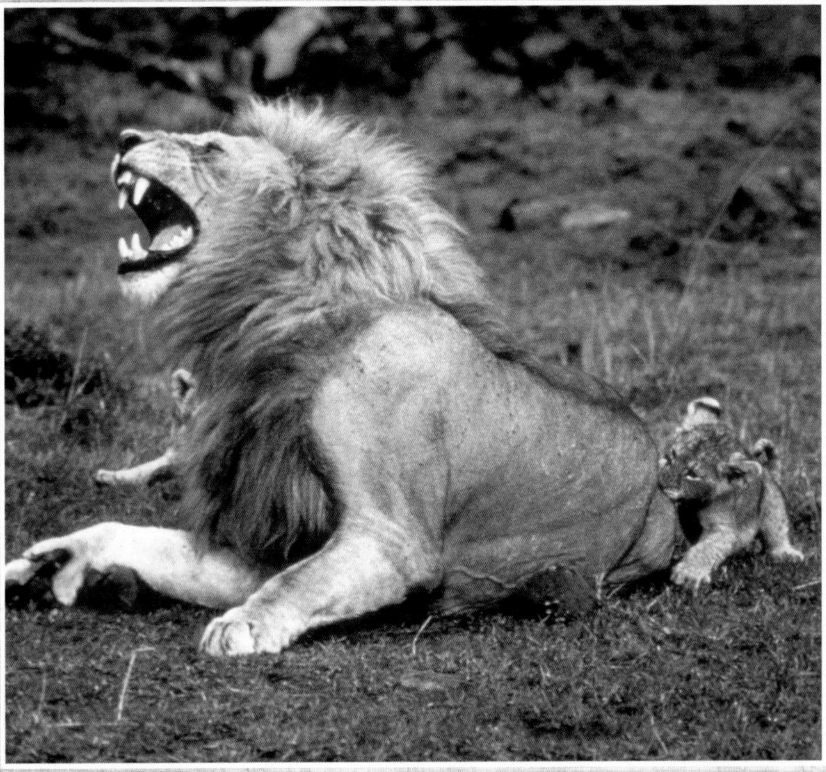

Home is where a father's strength
Surrounds, protects his own . . .

ANNA VALLANCE
from the poem "Home"

Musk Ox: When threatened by predators or bad weather, a herd of Musk Oxen closes ranks to form a defensive circle around their young, with the adults facing outwards, their curved horns providing a protective shield against all but the most aggressive wolves. During a blizzard, the musk oxen can stand in their tightly-bunched circle for days at a time, keeping each other warm through body heat, with the young safe and snug in the center of the circle.

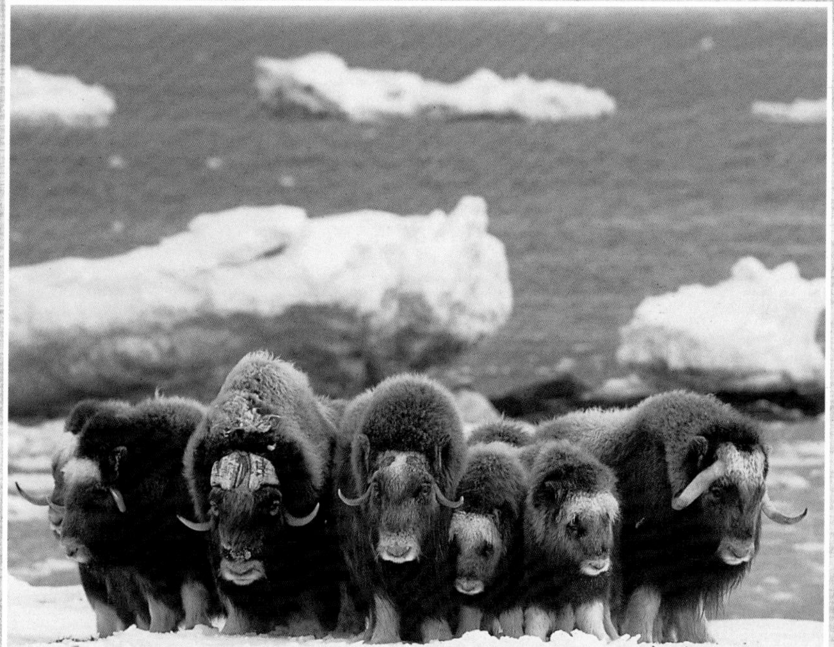

© Erwin & Peggy Bauer

I cannot think of any need in childhood as strong as the need for a father's protection.

SIGMUND FREUD (1856-1939)

Stickleback Fish: Stickleback males build nests that resemble tunnels. When building, the male will back up to look at the nest, then swim over to make adjustments. He'll add a stick or two, spitting water to move them into place. Once satisfied with his creation, the stickleback turns to finding a mate. He guides the female back into the "tunnel" to lay her eggs.

Once the eggs are laid, the male fans oxygen-filled water with his tail and fins to the eggs. When the eggs hatch, he tears off the top of the nest, leaving the bottom part as a cradle. The father guards the nest until the young are old enough to fend for themselves. If the young fish roam too far, he gathers them in his mouth and promptly spits them back into the nest.

There is nothing stronger in the world than gentleness.

HAN SUYIN
20th century Chinese author

Mugger Crocodile: The female lays her eggs in a nest cavity and covers them up with dirt. When the hatchlings start to call and chirp, the male and/or the female digs them out and carries them in their mouths to the nursery pools where they will be guarded for up to two years by one or both parents. Paternal instincts in male muggers are so well developed that some males have been known to claim exclusive rights to hatching the nest, which means that he will even chase away the mother.

How beautiful the world would be if all loved
one another as a father loves his own.

JOHN GRAY, PH.D.
20th century American author

Wild Horse: Stallions are very protective of their herd members. Ever on the alert, a stallion will stand watch over the herd while grabbing quick mouthfuls of grass. If danger approaches, a stallion will stand his ground, biting and kicking to protect his mares and foals if necessary, as the rest of the horses run to safety. Once the rest of the herd is safe, he too will then whirl and disappear.

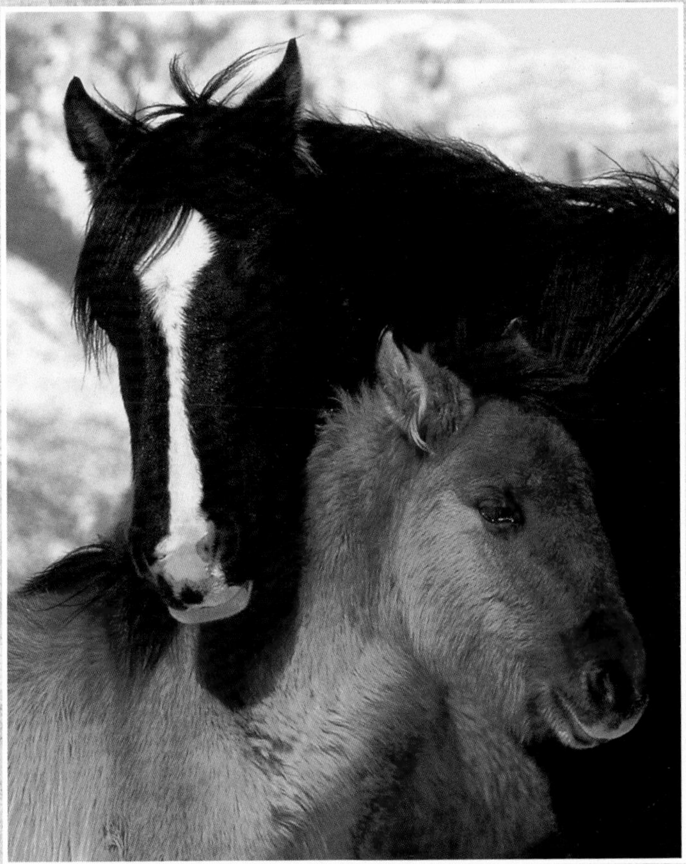

*There is something ultimate in a father's love,
something that cannot fail, something to be
believed against the whole world.*

FREDERICK W. FABER (1814-1863)
English Catholic priest and hymn writer

Marmoset: Marmoset fathers are highly devoted to their babies. The male even helps the female deliver them. He will bite off the umbilical cord, clean up the afterbirth, and wash each young monkey. As the young are born, the male places them on his back and every two or three hours, passes them back to his mate for feeding, who when finished with them hands them back to him. After three weeks, the babies start exploring and accept solid food when they are four weeks old. The male will often help them with their first mouthfuls of solid food by squeezing it through his fingers to make it easier to digest.

The name of father . . . another name for love.

FANNY FERN (1811-1872)
American author

Giraffe: The Giraffe is the tallest animal in the world, with females reaching about 15 feet in height. The mother does not lie down when she gives birth, so a calf's first experience in life is to fall head-first from a height of about seven feet. Although the mother does almost all of the calf-rearing, researchers have noted that males can be very attentive and caring toward the babies.

Children are love made visible.

Laysan Albatross: Albatross live at sea and find their meals in the open ocean. They come to land, on isolated islands, only to breed. Mating for life, a pair of Albatross parents meet at their breeding grounds, where the first activities involve building a nest. Once this is completed, a pair perform an elaborate courtship display. A single large egg weighing about one pound is laid and then incubated for 70 days by both parents. Once hatched, the chick is fed intermittently for up to ten months. One parent stays with the chick while the other collects food for it, feeding it by regurgitation. Parents can cover 9,500 miles during just one month of foraging to find food for their babies and themselves. When the chick is about seven pounds and big enough to repulse most predators, both parents go in search of food. For almost a year, both the father and the mother return occasionally to feed the huge, bloated, fluffy youngster, which lives mainly off its fat reserves. Once it leaves the nest, a young bird may not return to its home island to breed until it is at least five or sometimes up to ten years old.

Blessed indeed is the man who hears many gentle voices call him father!

LYDIA M. CHILD

Cooper's Hawk: The male Cooper's Hawk selects a nesting site and, sometimes assisted by the female, builds a platform nest of sticks and twigs up to 60 feet above the ground. The male brings food to the female while she is on the nest incubating the four to six eggs, and during the nestling stage. Once the young birds have fledged, they are still dependent on their parents for 30 to 40 days for food, as learning how to hunt and kill small mammals and birds is challenging and difficult to learn.

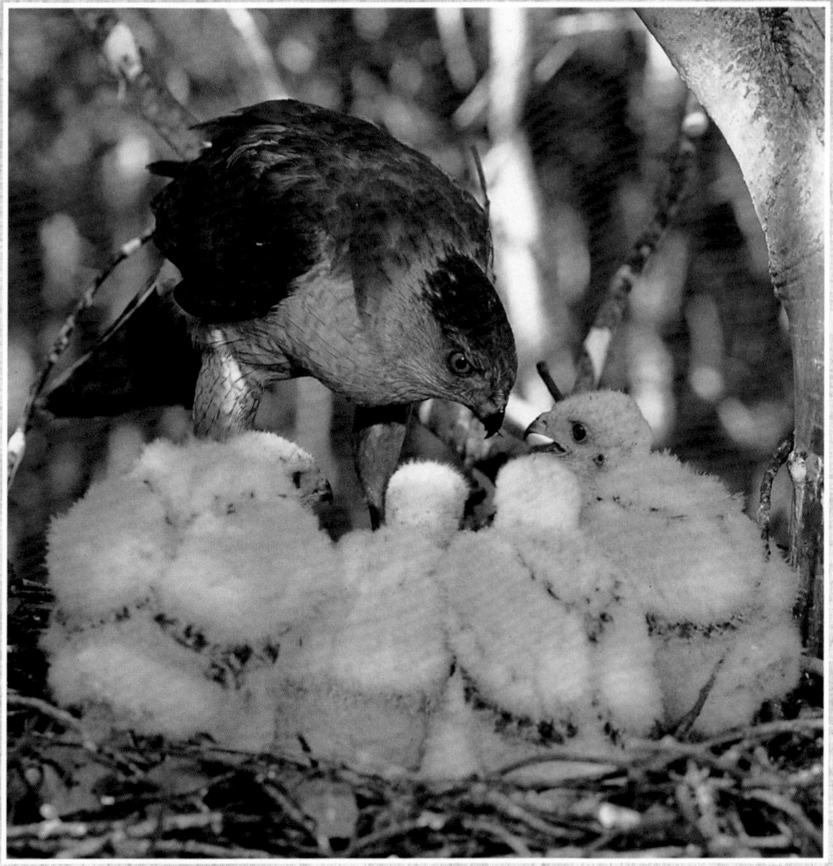

Children have never been very good at listening to their elders, but they have never failed to imitate them.

JAMES BALDWIN (1924-1987)
American author

Hoary Marmot: Hoary marmots are part of the same family of ground squirrels as the prairie dog. Each marmot family lives in a separate burrow, where they hibernate for about eight months each year. Like the prairie dog, both sexes nurture their offspring, especially while the pups are playing or exploring outside the burrow. A male will often gently groom any young pup.

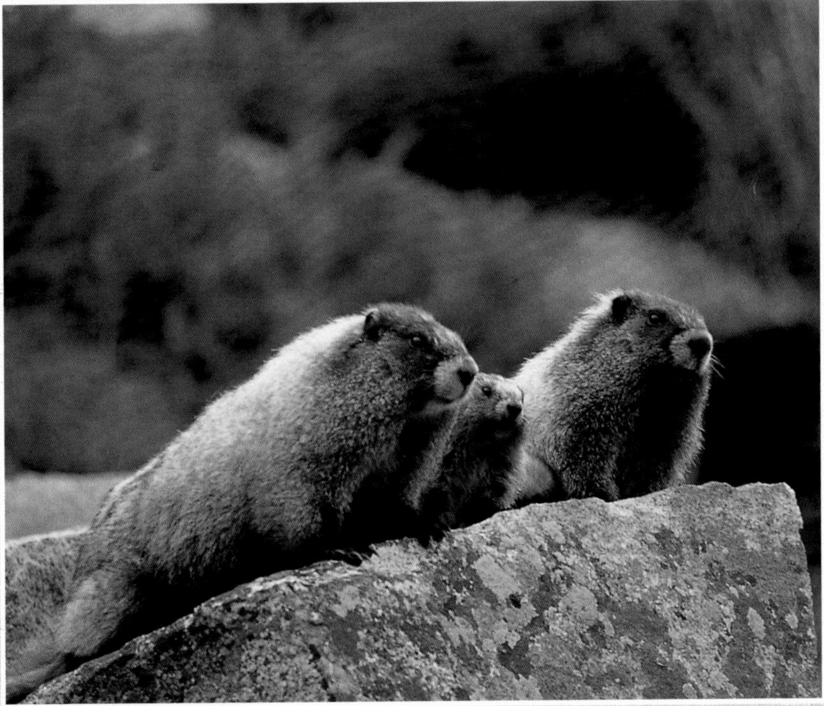

Children are intensely invested in getting their way.
They will devote more emotional and intellectual
energy to winning arguments than parents
ever will, and are almost always better rested.

JEAN CALLAHAN
20th century American journalist

Northern Cardinal: The male cardinal delivers food to the female while she incubates the two to five eggs. Once the eggs hatch, both parents bring the chicks food. Once the birds have fledged, the male continues to deliver meals to the first brood while the female incubates a second clutch.

The quickest way to get a child's attention is to sit down and look comfortable.

LANE OLINGHOUSE
20th century American writer

Chimpanzee: Chimpanzees, having the closest DNA to human's than any other animal, seem to show similar emotions toward their young as do people. Adult males display a great deal of patience and interest in pesky youngsters wanting to play games, wrestle, tickle, and poke. They often engage the youngsters in wild bouts of climbing and chase, and seem to enjoy it as much as the young chimps.

Children seldom misquote you. In fact, they usually repeat word for word what you shouldn't have said.

ANONYMOUS

Coyote: At three weeks, pups begin to eat food that the parents regurgitate. Once strong enough, pups play outside the den, guarded by both parents. When the pups are eight- to ten-weeks old, the whole family goes on hunting trips, where the pups learn hunting and survival skills from both parents. The pups leave their parents' protection in the fall when they are about 6 to 7 months old.

Are you lost, daddy, I asked tenderly.
Shut up, he explained.

RING LARDNER, SR. (1885-1933)
American humorist

Canada Goose: Male-female bonds are permanent in Canada geese, and the pair often travels with young from the previous year until they are ready to nest again. The female constructs a nest lined with down from her own breast and commonly lays five to six cream-colored eggs. Once incubation begins, the goose rarely leaves her nest for the 25 to 28 days required for the young to hatch. The gander stands guard and courageously attacks any creature he perceives as a threat. Newly-hatched young are precocial, which means that they are covered with down and able to follow their parents and feed soon after hatching. The new family is almost an inseparable troupe; usually Mom leads the way, followed by the young, with Dad bringing up the rear.

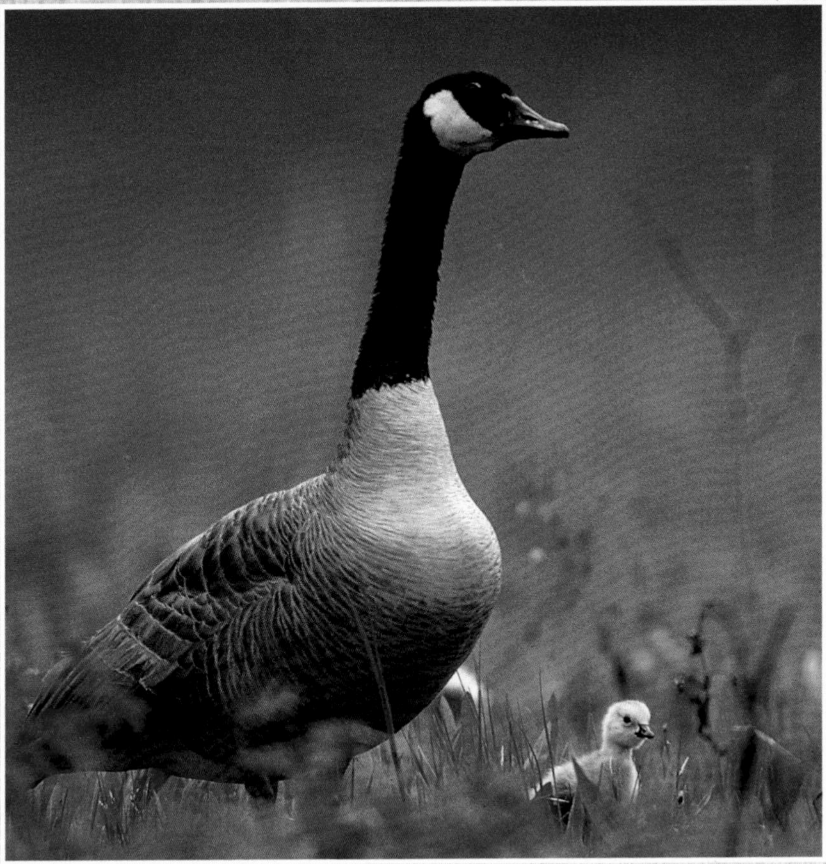

The impressions made by a father's voice can set in motion an entire trend of life.

GORDON MACDONALD
20th century author

Whiskered Tern: Each pair of terns has a territory within the breeding colony where they scrape a shallow depression in the earth. The female and male share in the incubation of the eggs. Once hatched, the male does all of the fishing during the first five to seven days, supplying food for himself, the female and the young. At about a week, both parents go out to catch fish for the young, who start to wander away from the nest. A parent will then bring a fish directly to a young bird, who eats it whole.

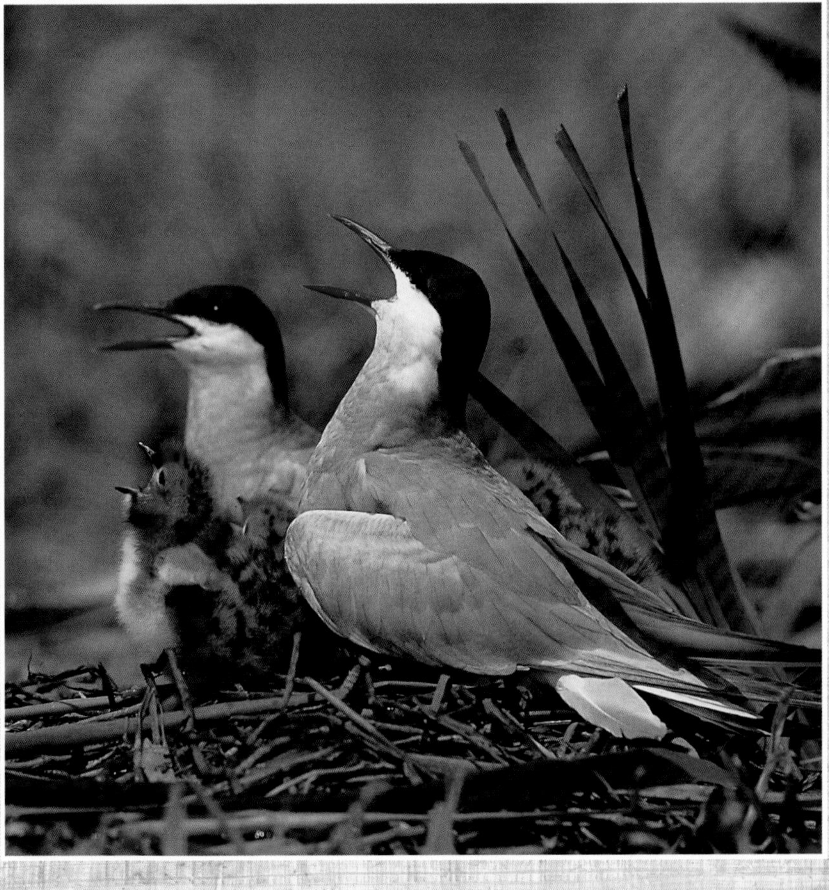

One father is more than a hundred schoolmasters.

ENGLISH PROVERB

Least Bittern: The least bittern's nest, constructed by both parents, is typically a platform with a shallow hollow located near or over water. The eggs are incubated by both parents, and once hatched, the chicks are fed regurgitated food.

My father didn't tell me how to live;
he lived and let me watch him do it.

CLARENCE BUDINGTON KELLAND, (1881-1964)
American author

Elk: As the fall mating season approaches, bulls form harems of cows consisting on average of six females and four calves, which they will defend with their large size and aggressive nature. Although the female gives birth and nurses her calf away from any males, an elk calf will graze regularly with the adults once it is two- to three-months old.

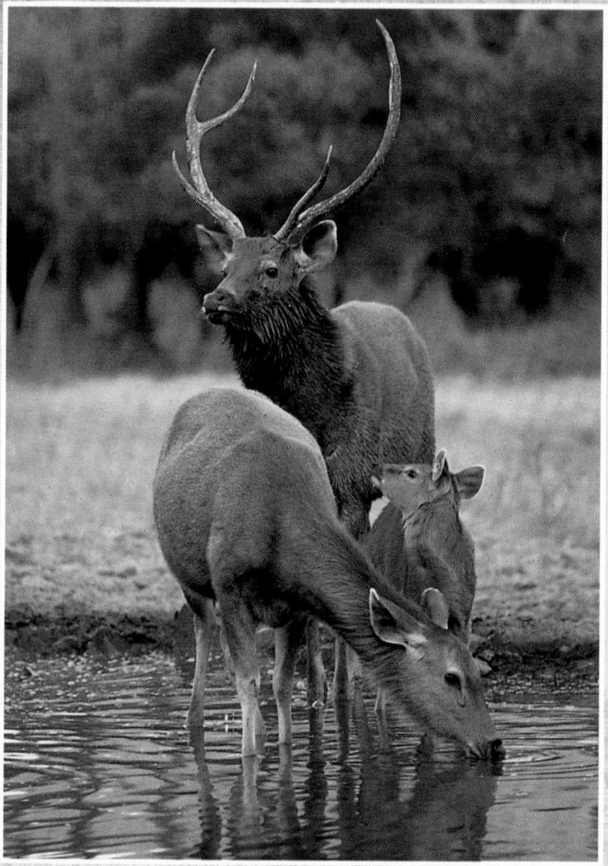

*Each day of our lives we make deposits
into the memory banks of our children.*

DR. CHARLES R. SWINDOLL
20th century American author and minister

Beaver: A beaver family consists of the mated pair, who have been together for many years, and their off-spring, who stay with them for almost two years. Each year, the female gives birth to two to nine kits in very early spring. Once weaned, all members of the family bring vegetation to the kits, who remain in the lodge. By summer, the kits are able to swim well enough to leave the lodge and forage with the family, where the young beavers' education begins immediately. Even tiny beaver kits gnaw at sticks and carry building material when the family makes a repair to their lodge or dam. In November, the parents will drive out the two-year old beavers who must leave and find mates and streams of their own.

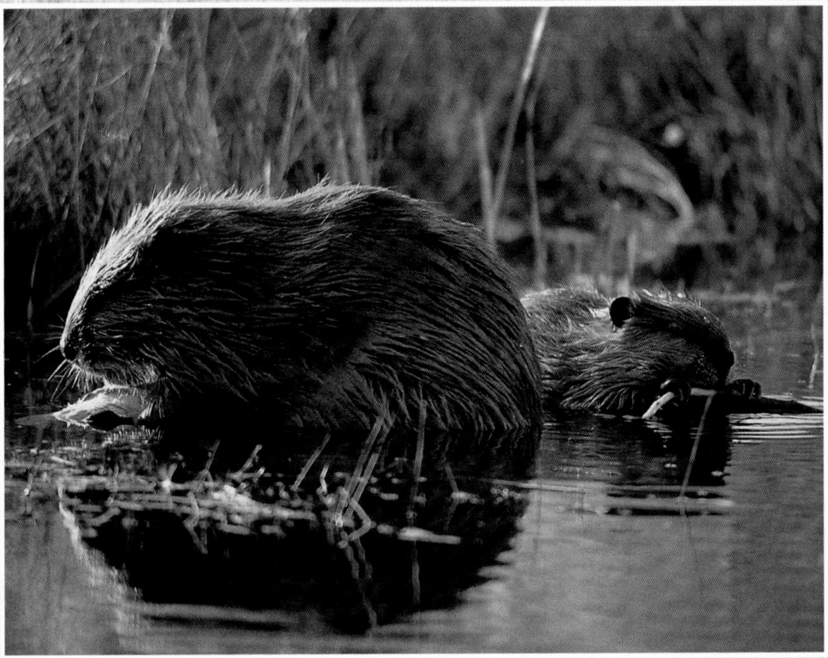

It doesn't matter who my father was;
it matters who I remember he was.

ANNE SEXTON
American poet

Poison Dart Frog: The female lays her eggs in small batches, usually in an upturned leaf which has collected rain water. The eggs and young tadpoles are then guarded by the male. When the tadpoles reach a certain size, they slither up the male's back and attach themselves to a patch of sticky mucus secreted from glands in his skin. He then carries the tadpoles to a larger, more permanent area of water where they complete their development.

*His heritage to his children wasn't words
or possessions, but an unspoken treasure,
the treasure of his example
as a man and a father.*

WILL ROGERS, JR. (1879-1935)
American actor

Red Fox: The male red fox is an attentive mate and father. His job is providing the female with food every four to six hours for the three to four weeks she is in the den nursing the newborn cubs. The father will even go without food himself until she is full. When the cubs are being weaned, both parents will regurgitate food for the cubs. When the weaning is completed, both parents hunt at night to bring the cubs earthworms, small mammals, and birds to eat. Parents eventually start reducing food as a tactic to get the pups moving away from the den, and it's the father that takes the lead with this strategy. Dad doesn't just leave the young hungry, however; he helps teach survival skills. He buries surplus food close to the den and disguises it with leaves and twigs. This technique teaches the pups to sniff and forage.

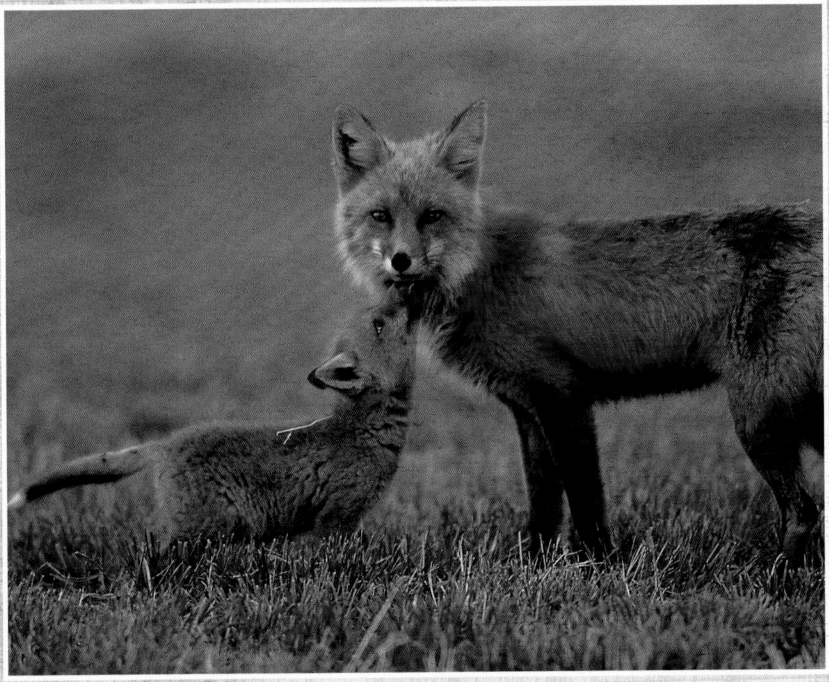

Life doesn't come with an Instruction Book;
that's why we have fathers.

H. JACKSON BROWN , JR.
20th century American author

Chimpanzee: Young male chimpanzees spend less time with their mothers as they grow older, and instead follow after adult males. In adolescence, "teenage" male chimps tag along with adult males patrolling the perimeters of their home territory, trying to detect and pursue chimpanzees of other communities. In this photograph, the young chimp is being taught to "fish" for termites to eat, using a reed that termites find tasty.

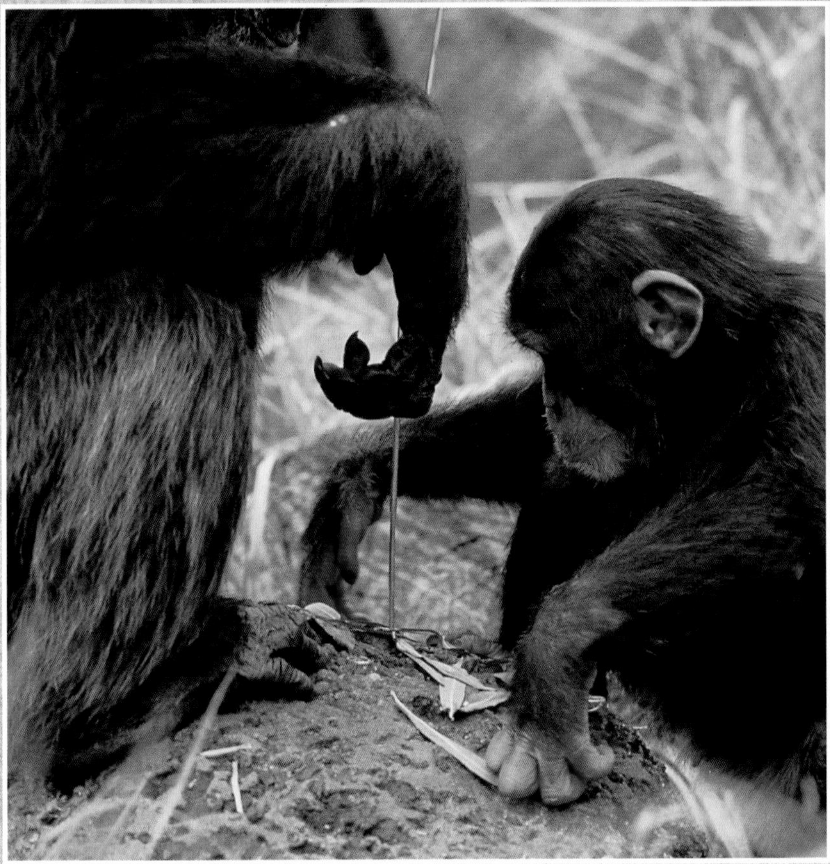

A father's lessons are gifts that last a lifetime.

JOAN AHO RYAN

Bald Eagle: Bald Eagles build the largest nest of any bird. Composed of sticks, nests typically exceed three feet across and two feet in depth. Nests are situated on strong branches near the tops of huge trees, and are perennial, meaning that the eagles will return to the same nest each year and continue to build and reconstruct it. Some eagles have been known to use the same nest for over 35 years! Bald eagles mate for life, and both birds protect the nest territory from other eagles and predators. Incubation duties are also shared. Both male and female eagles are caring and cautious parents. To protect the young from accidental injury from their razor-sharp talons, the adults close their feet and talons while in the nest and walk on "balled up" feet around the young and eggs, cautiously and gently moving about to feed and brood the young. The male provides the majority of the food needed by his rapidly-growing family in the early weeks of growth.

*I don't mind looking into the mirror
and seeing my father.*

MICHAEL DOUGLAS
American actor

Gray wolf: Father wolves have been known to attempt to nurse the pups after their mother has died. The whole pack—males and females—help feed and care for the young once they are weaned. By the time they are eight to ten weeks old, the pups are strong enough to leave the den altogether. The youngsters spend the days frolicking, wrestling together, and pouncing on small creatures such as mice. When the pups are about six months old, the pack returns to its normal nomadic lifestyle, and the young wolves learn how to hunt in earnest. Unless they stay as helpers, the young leave when they are one to two years old to try to establish themselves in their own territories.

A father is someone you look up to
no matter how tall you are.

ANONYMOUS

King Penguin: The male and female King Penguin join in a dedicated partnership for raising young that requires ultra-responsible vigilance for nearly a year that continues throughout winter. They take turns incubating their one egg, with the male taking first turn while the female has two weeks off after laying the egg. For the next six weeks, each parent spends about five days at a time incubating while the other goes to feed. The parent on duty holds the egg on its large webbed feet and engulfs it in a fold of belly skin. Once the chick hatches, it grows rapidly and reaches the size of its parents within a few weeks. Chicks, however, spend their first year inside a suit of frothy, fuzzy brown-gray feathers that are not waterproof. As the parents go off to feed in the worst of winter, the chicks huddle together for warmth and may lose nearly half their body weight. As winter nears its end, the parents start regularly feeding the chicks again, as the young are totally dependent on their parents to feed them regurgitated food until they molt out of their baby plumage.

As parents, we never stand so tall as when we stoop to help our children.

DR. ANTHONY P. WITHAM
Founder of the American Family Institute

Greater Flamingo: Both the male and female build the nest together, a mound of mud about a foot in diameter. They construct a circular trench around the nest to protect it from flooding. Both parents incubate their single egg, which hatches after about 30 days. Flamingo chicks are at first completely dependent on their parents. They cannot feed themselves until the complex filters inside their beaks have fully developed, and so the parents feed them a mush of partly-digested algae. Around 10 weeks of age, a chick can fly and will join its parents in nightly journeys in search of the richest feeding grounds.

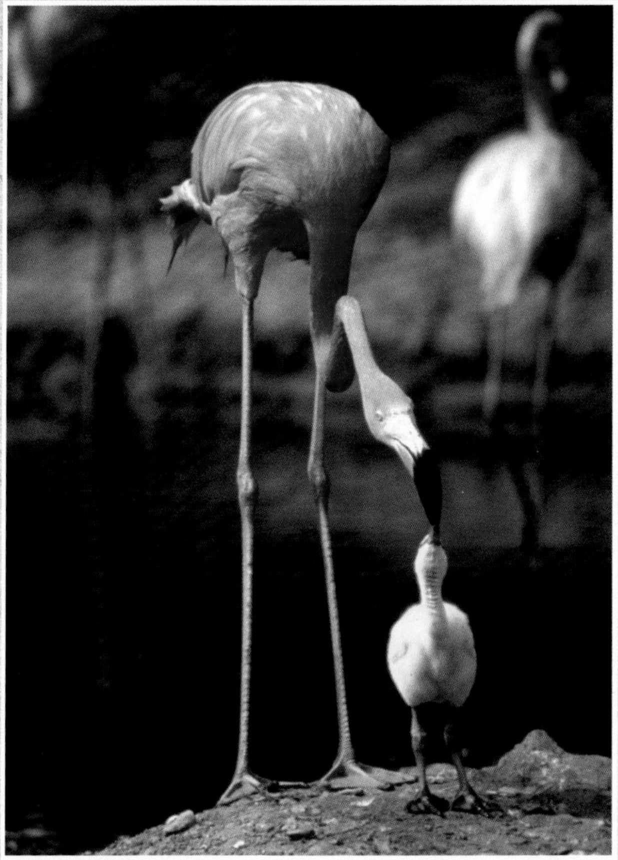

Nothing can ever replace the wisdom,
guidance and love of a good father.

GEORGE WEBSTER DOUGLAS
20th century American writer

Black and White Colobus Monkey: Colobus monkeys spend nearly all of their time in the tops of trees where leaves, their favorite food, are within easy reach. Infant colobus monkeys will cling to either the father's or the mother's stomach, as both the male and female take part in parenting. Colobus troops are highly social, and the infant may be handled by all members of the troop. A strong male acts as the lead animal; he threatens enemies and if necessary covers the retreat of the troop.

It is a wise father that knows his own child.

WILLIAM SHAKESPEARE

Gorillas: Gorillas roam the rain forest in family groups of usually five to ten members, comprising a dominant male, females, and their young. Young gorillas are extremely playful. They chase each other, climb, wrestle, and often pester the adults. When relaxed, the dominant male, known as the silverback, is the center of attraction for the young. It is common to see silverbacks gently grooming and playing with infants. He lets the young climb on him, pull his hair, and punch his massive bulk with their tiny fists.

Gorillas are solely vegetarian and must move every day to a new feeding area in the forest. The silverback leads his family group and decides where they feed and sleep. Although a silverback typically weighs over 300 pounds and stands over five feet tall, his great bulk and muscular power is only used when a young male challenges his status. Then the opponents try to intimidate each other by roaring, tearing at vegetation, running sideways, and beating their chests. This chest-thumping show is mostly a very successful bluff, however.

*A father is neither an anchor to hold us back,
nor a sail to take us there, but a guiding light
whose love shows us the way.*

GEORGE WEBSTER DOUGLAS
20th century American writer

Ostrich: The male ostrich scrapes out a shallow nest in the sandy soil, and a female lays four to eight eggs in it. Then the male courts several other females, who also lay their eggs in his nest. Each hen lays every other day until there is a clutch of about 25 eggs. Nest duties are shared by the male and the most dominant female. She incubates the eggs by day; he takes over at night. In about six weeks, the chicks are ready to hatch, and they call from within the thick-shelled eggs. Only about half of the eggs hatch. Ostrich chicks can feed themselves as soon as they hatch, but are in danger from predators such as foxes and jackals. The male and the dominant female gather the chicks into a creche and watch over them constantly. If they are threatened, one bird may attempt to distract and draw off the predator. The parents also shade the chicks from the sun, and lead them to food and water. Although only about one chick in ten survives to be one year old, an adult ostrich has little to fear from predators.

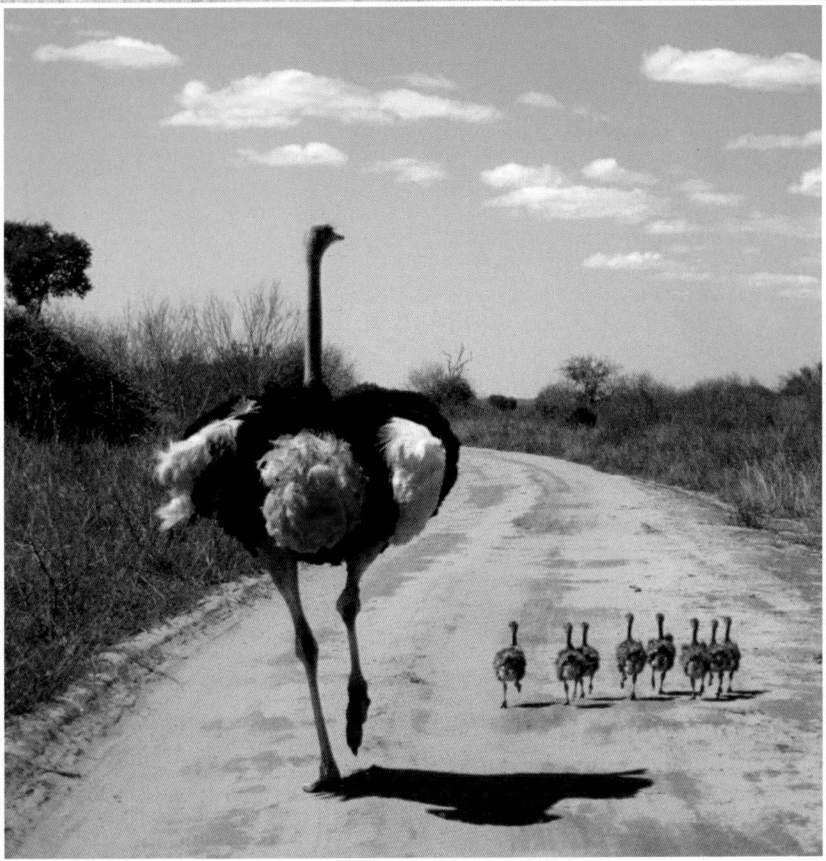

A father is . . .
a hand on your shoulder through every storm.

CHRIS GALLATIN
American poet

Japanese Macaque: Japanese macaque monkeys live in groups of 30 to 40 members, made up of five or six males, about ten related females, and their offspring. They live farther north than any other monkey or ape, and are the only monkey found in Japan. Most infant care is given by the mother, but as a baby grows, the entire family is tolerant of and caring toward the youngster. All the males of the troop have strong ties with the young, and strive to protect them. Males will also often busy themselves with carrying and grooming the young. If one male with a baby in its grasp meets another male that appears aggressive, he may offer the baby to the competitor as a distraction or a buffer, thereby preventing a fight.

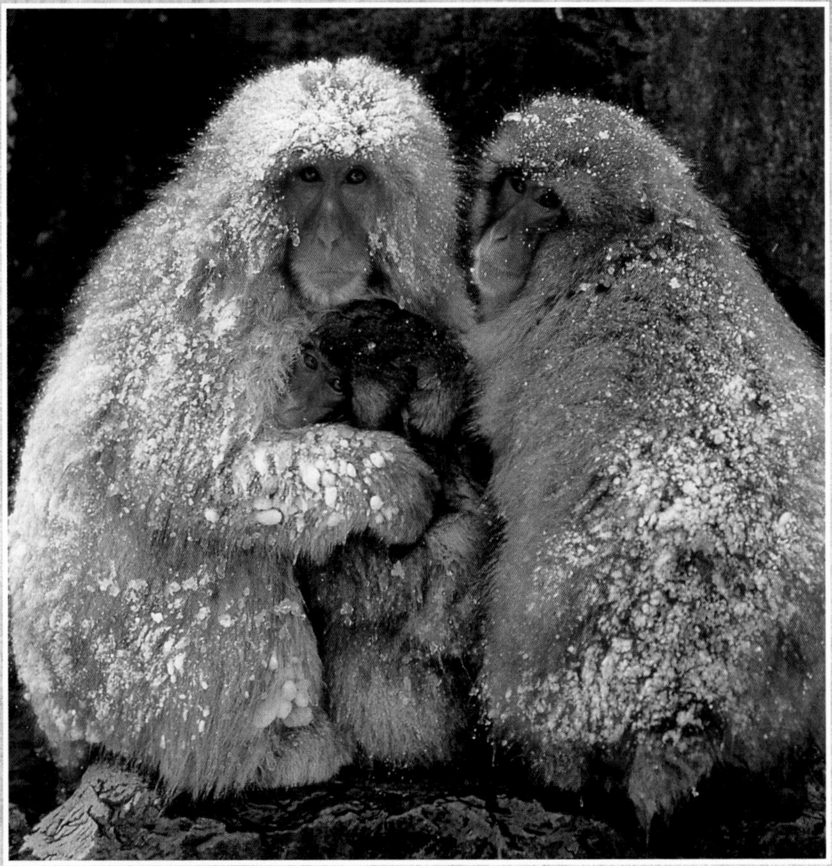

You know, fathers just have a way of putting everything together.

ERIKA COSBY
Daughter of Bill Cosby

Ring-Tailed Lemur: The lemurs of Madagascar socialize in groups of 15 to 30 individuals, and are among the few primates able to trust newborn babies to other members of the group. Male lemurs do their best to protect the group and will carry any baby lemur about, fondling it as though enormously interested and reliable. He will also offer an insect or other favorite food to the infant he is carrying, who may or may not be his biological child.

By profession I am a soldier and take pride in that fact.
But I am prouder—infinitely prouder—to be a father.

GENERAL DOUGLAS MACARTHUR (1880-1964)

Gray Wolf: Growing wolf pups enjoy a carefree life playing and exploring in the home area. The dominant male, who is also the father, or another member of the pack keeps constant watch on the curious and playful puppies. Every animal in the pack will respond to the needs of the young, whether by regurgitating food or protecting them from danger.

*I have learnt too much of the heart of man
not to be certain that it is only in the bosom
of my family that I shall find happiness.*

FRANCOIS DOMINIQUE TOUSSAINT-L'OUVERTINE (1743-1803)

Chimpanzee: Contact is an essential element of chimpanzee behavior. It plays an important part in social situations whether the chimpanzee is excited, afraid, playing, or relaxing. A pat, embrace, or kiss relieves the fears and frustrations of an infant.

We may find some of our best friends
in our own blood.

RALPH WALDO EMERSON (1803-1882)

Gray Fox: Researchers have observed male foxes exhibiting much excitement about their pups, playing with them endlessly. While the vixen is in the den for the first three to four weeks after the cubs are born, the male hunts and brings back food for her. Later, when the cubs are being weaned, both parents will regurgitate food for them, which will continue until the cubs have learned to hunt for themselves.

Home is the place there's no place like.

CHARLES SCHULZ (1922-2000)
American cartoonist

Night Monkey: South American night monkeys have a strong pair bond that is shown by their behavior when they are going to sleep. The two sit side by side and entwine their tails before nodding off. Females are pregnant or nursing young almost every year, so they are in need of a supportive spouse. Males of a troop will commonly "babysit" high in the forest canopy. They will haul the young along with them even though the burden slows their progress and reduces their opportunities to eat. The child-free females catch more than their normal share of insects and reach laden fruit trees to feast before the males with young arrive. The females can also move more swiftly from predators than they could if they had infants in their arms.

A man finds out what is meant by a "spitting image"
when he tries to feed cereal to his infant.

Blue-footed Booby: After mating, a curious ritual of symbolic nest-building takes place between the male and female, which seems to serve no practical purpose. One or the other of the blue-footed booby pair picks up a twig or stone and places it where the eggs will be laid. When the female is ready to lay, the nest material is scraped away so she can lay her eggs on the bare ground.

Unlike most birds, the blue-footed booby lacks brooding patches, areas of bare skin that transmit heat from the bird's body to the eggs. Instead, the booby parents alternately incubate the eggs beneath their broad, webbed, blue feet. Their feet have an increased blood supply which conveys heat to the eggs, maintaining a constant temperature of 103°F. When the chicks start to hatch, the booby supports the eggs on the tops of its feet until the chicks are free from their shells. Chicks feed from both the father and mother, thrusting their bills inside their parents' to obtain regurgitated fish.

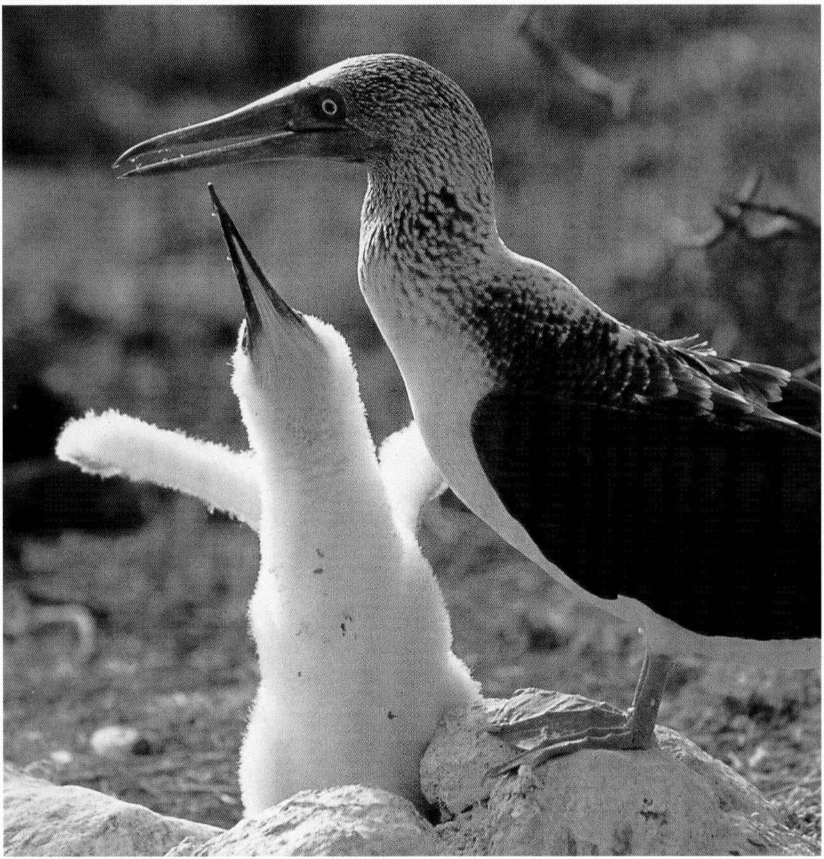

A father who will pursue infant care with ease and proficiency is simply a father who has never been told to believe he couldn't.

MICHAEL K. MEYERHOFF
American writer

Western Grebes: Male and female grebes woo each other through a series of elaborate and graceful courtship dances. Once their partnership is established, the parents share all the work of raising a family. The birds build a nest from aquatic plant material anchored to reeds — the nests of a colony of 100 or more pairs form a floating island where they are secure from land predators. Both parents incubate the three or four eggs, taking turns to go and feed. The eggs hatch after three weeks and the chicks leave the nest soon afterwards to swim with their parents. Both adults feed them fish and insects, and carry them on their backs. The grebe chicks grow quickly through the summer, and soon learn to dive. At any hint of danger, the parents dive with a splash, a signal for the youngsters to follow and seek safety underwater. The youngsters are independent by late fall.

*A father's love warms the hearts
of his children forever.*

ANONYMOUS

Lion: Lions are the most social of the cat family. They live in prides consisting of one or two males, up to seven females, and 14 or 15 cubs of different ages. Mom leaves the pride to give birth alone. Once the cubs are big enough to follow their mother, she will take them to the pride and introduce them to their father. Adult lions are fond of cubs, and the introduction of new ones is an occasion for a good deal of solicitous examination.

Bibliography

Grateful acknowledgment is made to the authors and publishers for use of the following material. If notified, the publisher will be pleased to rectify an omission in future editions.

Allen, Jessica (ed.). *Quotable Men of the Twentieth Century*. W. Morrow, New York, NY, 1999.

Amazing Animals, Library of Curious and Unusual Facts. Time-Life Books, Alexandria, VA, 1990.

Baldwin, James. *Nobody Knows My Name: More Notes of a Native Son*. Dial Press, New York, NY, 1961.

Bateman, G. *Encyclopedia of Mammals*. Facts on File, Inc., New York, NY, 1984.

Black, David. *Animal Wonders of the World*. Orbis Publishing Ltd., London, UK, 1981.

Brown Jr., H. Jackson. *Life's Little Instruction Book*. Rutledge Hill Press, Nashville, TN, 1991.

Callahan, Jean. "Single Parents." *Parenting Magazine*. February, 1992.

Cosby, Bill; introduction and afterword by Alvin F. Poussaint. *Fatherhood*. Doubleday, Garden City, NY, 1986.

Dickering, Fran. *Encyclopedia of Animals in Nature, Myth and Spirit*. Element Children's Books, Boston, MA, 1999.

Estes, Richard D. *The Behavior Guide to African Mammals*. University of California Press, Berkley, CA, 1991.

Freedman, Russell. *Animal Fathers*. Holiday House, New York, NY, 1976.

Goetz, David (ed.). *Leadership Meditations: Reflections for Leaders in All Walks of Life*. Tyndale House Publishers, Wheaton, IL, 2001.

Grzimek, B. *Grzimek's Encyclopedia of Mammals*. McGraw-Hill, Inc., Muncher, West Germany, 1988.

Kaplan, Louise J. *Oneness and Separateness: From Infant to Individual*. Simon and Schuster, New York, NY, 1978.

Lansky, Bruce (compiled by). *Familiarity Breeds Children*. Meadowbrook Press, New York, NY, 1994.

McLellan, Vern (compiled by). *The Complete Book of Practical Proverbs and Wacky Wit.* Tyndale House Publishing, Wheaton, IL, 1996.

Mead, Lucy (compiled by). *Fathers Are Special.* Gramercy Books, New York, NY, 2000.

Milne, Lorus J. and Margery Milne. *The Behavior and Learning of Animal Babies.* The Globe Pequot Press, Chester, CT, 1988.

National Geographic Book of Mammals, Volume One. National Geographic Society, Washington D.C., 1986.

Nerburn, Kent. *Letters to My Son: Reflections on Becoming a Man.* New World Library, San Rafael, CA, 1993.

Prochnow, Herbert V. and Herbt V. Prochnow, Jr. *A Treasure Chest of Quotations for All Occasions.* Harper & Row, New York, NY, 1983.

Pruett, Kyle D. *The Nurturing Father: Journey Toward the Complete Man.* Warner Books, New York, NY, 1987.

Reader's Digest Quotable Quotes: Wit and Wisdom for All Occasions from America's Most Popular Magazine. Reader's Digest, Pleasantville, NY, 1997.

Ryan, Joan Aho. *Lessons from Dad: A Tribute to Fatherhood.* Health Communications, Deerfield Beach, FL, 1997.

Slater, Professor Peter J. B. (ed.). *Encyclopedia of Animal Behavior.* Facts on File Publications, New York, NY, 1987.

Sullivan, Bridget (ed.). *Fathers.* Andrews McMeel Publishing, Kansas City, MO, 1996.

Swindoll, Charles R. *The Strong Family.* Zondervan Publishing House, Grand Rapids, MI, 1994.

Thoughts to Share with a Wonderful Father: A Collection from Blue Mountain Arts. Blue Mountain Press, Boulder, CO, 1999.

Touchstones: A Book of Daily Meditations for Men. Hazelden, Center City, MN, 1991.

The Wildlife Year: Life Cycles of Nature Around the World. The Reader's Digest Association Ltd., London, 1991.